A VISIT TO
Puerto Rico

REVISED AND UPDATED

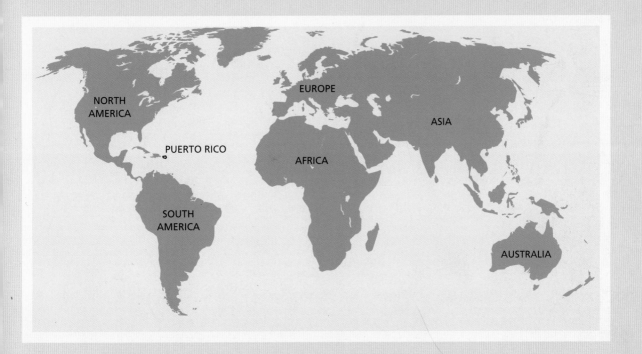

NORTH
AMERICA

PUERTO RICO

SOUTH
AMERICA

EUROPE

AFRICA

ASIA

AUSTRALIA

Leila Merrell Foster

Heinemann Library
Chicago, Illinois

© 2001, 2009 Heinemann Library
a division of Pearson Inc.
Chicago, Illinois

Customer Service 888-454-2279
Visit our website at www.heinemannraintree.com

Designed by Joanna Hinton-Malivoire
Printed in China by South China Printing Company Limited

13 12 11 10 09
10 9 8 7 6 5 4 3 2 1

New edition ISBN-10: 1-4329-1279-8 (hardcover), 1-4329-1298-4 (paperback)
New edition ISBN-13: 978-1-4329-1279-6 (hardcover), 978-1-4329-1298-7 (paperback)

The Library of Congress has cataloged the first edition as follows:
Foster, Leila Merrell.
       Puerto Rico / Leila Merrell Foster.
            p.cm. – (A visit to)
       Includes bibliographical references and index.
       Summary: An introduction to the land, culture, and people of Puerto Rico.
       ISBN 1-57572-381-6 (library binding)
       1. Puerto Rico—Description and travel—Juvenile literature. [1. Puerto Rico.] I. Title. II. Series.

F1965.3 .F67 2000
972.95—dc21

                                                        00-02953

Acknowledgments
The publishers are grateful to the following for permission to reproduce copyright material:
© Corbis pp. **6** (Bob Krist), **7** (Tom Bean), **9** (Stephanie Maze), **11** (Franz-Marc Frei, **13** (Tony Arruza), **14** (Tony Arruza), **15** (Bob Krist), **18** (Tony Arruza), **19** (Macduff Everton), **22** (Stephanie Maze), **24** (Stephanie Maze), **25** (Tony Arruza), **26** (Tony Arruza), **27** (Tony Arruza), **28** (Bob Krist), **29** (James Marshall); © David R. Frazier Photolibrary, Inc. p. **16** (Alamy); © DDB Stock pp. **20** (Jack Messler), **21** (Suzanne Murphy-Larronde), **23** (Robert Fried); © Jupiter Images p. **12** (FoodPix/Gentl & Hyers); © Lucid Images p. **10** (PictureQuest/Mark Downey); © Photolibrary Group p. **5** (Glow Images [Masterfile]); © Tony Stone Images pp. **8** (Mark Lewis), **17** (Robert Frereck).

Cover photograph reproduced with permission of © Lonely Planet (John Elk III).

Every effort has been made to contact copyright holders of any material reproduced in this book. Any omissions will be rectified in subsequent printings if notice is given to the publisher.

Contents

Any words appearing in bold, **like this**, are explained in the Glossary.

Puerto Rico

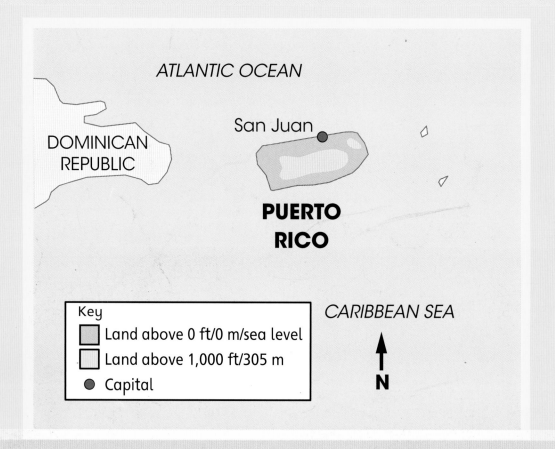

ATLANTIC OCEAN

DOMINICAN
REPUBLIC

San Juan

**PUERTO
RICO**

CARIBBEAN SEA

Key
- Land above 0 ft/0 m/sea level
- Land above 1,000 ft/305 m
- ● Capital

N

Puerto Rico is a group of islands in the **Caribbean Sea**. It is miles from the United States **mainland**, but it is still part of the U.S.

There is one big main island and a number of smaller islands in Puerto Rico. It is a beautiful place where people like to go on vacation.

Puerto rico means "rich **port**" in Spanish.

The main island has rocky hills and some mountains. It has good **ports** for boats. The beaches are sandy.

The weather is warm. Some rain falls almost every day. There is a mountain **rain forest** in Puerto Rico. It has waterfalls, animals, and big plants.

The rain forest in Puerto Rico is called **El Yunque**.

Landmarks

The **capital** of Puerto Rico is San Juan. The best-known landmark is a fort called El Morro. People from Spain built the fort hundreds of years ago.

The Arecibo
telescope is
1000 feet across.

Puerto Rico has one of the largest **radio
telescopes** in the world. It is used to study
stars and gas clouds. It is in a big hole in
the ground.

Homes

Most Puerto Ricans live in cities. In the **capital**, some people live in houses or apartment buildings. There are some old buildings and many new ones, too.

In the country and in the mountains, houses may be small. In the old days, houses were made of wood. They had roofs of **palm** leaves. Today most houses are made of **concrete**.

Some homes in the country are in the hills.

Food

Rice and beans and fish are favorite foods. **Spices** such as hot peppers are used to flavor foods. Many Puerto Rican foods first came from Spain and Africa.

Fruits and vegetables are sold in markets.

Many kinds of fruits grow in Puerto Rico. There are pineapples, bananas, and oranges. Coconuts also grow in Puerto Rico. People can buy them at fruit stands.

Clothes

Puerto Ricans usually dress in warm-weather clothes. Children often wear T-shirts or shirts with short sleeves, and shorts or jeans.

14

Sometimes people dress up in special clothes. The boys wear straw hats and cotton shirts and pants. Girls wear ruffled blouses and skirts.

Work

In the cities, many Puerto Ricans work in factories. They make clothes, medicines, and computer parts.

In the country, farmers grow **sugarcane.**
Coffee is also an important crop. Many
people also work in fishing. They catch a
lot of lobsters.

Transportation

Cruise ships stop at San Juan. They bring **tourists** to the islands. Airplanes and ships connect Puerto Rico with other countries.

The cities of Puerto Rico have wide streets to drive along.

Puerto Rico has good roads. They stretch from **coast** to coast on the main island. People use cars, buses, trucks, and cabs to get around.

Languages

People from Spain **settled** Puerto Rico and most people speak Spanish. Puerto Rico is part of the United States, so many people also speak English.

Spanish uses some of the same letters as English. Sometimes people speak a mixture of Spanish and English called "Spanglish."

School

Children must go to school from the ages of 6 to 16. The lessons are taught in Spanish. Children also learn English. Many children wear school uniforms.

There are many universities and colleges in Puerto Rico. People can go to study there after they have finished **secondary school**.

Free Time

Baseball is a favorite sport in Puerto Rico. Many Puerto Ricans have been stars of major league teams. Roberto Clemente was a famous Puerto Rican baseball player. He had 3,000 base hits.

Water sports such as fishing, **surfing**, and swimming are popular. Many people **scuba dive** to get a close look at fish and sea life.

Celebrations

During some **festivals**, people dress up in costumes. There are parades, rides, dancing, and singing. Puerto Ricans celebrate the Fourth of July and Presidents' Day, too.

Most people in Puerto Rico are Roman Catholic, so religious holidays are very important. Some holidays celebrate special days of people called **saints**.

The Arts

Music and dance in Puerto Rico mix Spanish, **native** Puerto Rican, and African beats. There are many **folk dances** that people still dance.

28

Many musicians play drums, **gourds**, and guitars. Some famous musicians got their start by playing on the street.

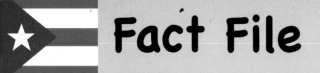

Fact File

Name	The Commonwealth of Puerto Rico is the country's full name.
Capital	Puerto Rico's **capital** is San Juan.
Language	The people speak Spanish and English.
Population	There are about four million people living in Puerto Rico.
Money	Puerto Rican money is called the dollar.
Religion	Most Puerto Ricans are Roman Catholic.
Products	**Sugarcane** and coffee are important crops. Chemicals, food, machines, and computers are sent to other countries.

Words you can learn

hola (OH-la)	hello
adiós (ah-dee-OS)	goodbye
sí (see)	yes
no (no)	no
gracias (GRAH-see-ahs)	thank you
por favor (pore fah-VOR)	please
uno/una (oo-noh/oo-nah)	one
dos (dos)	two
tres (trays)	three

Glossary

capital important city where the government is based

Caribbean Sea sea south of Florida that is part of the Atlantic Ocean and that is near Central and South America

coast land at the edge of an ocean

concrete material that is mixed with stone, sand, and water that is used to make buildings

cruise ship big ship that takes people who are on vacation from place to place

El Yunque the mountain rain forest in Puerto Rico. (You say El YOONG-kay.)

festival party held by a whole town or country

folk dance dance that people in a country have danced for a long time

gourd large fruit with a hard shell that can be dried to make cups, bowls, or musical instruments

mainland main part of the United States

native people who live in a place before other people come to settle there

palm tree without branches that has large leaves at the top and that grows well in warm places

port place where boats can stay

radio telescope special instrument used to study the stars with radio waves

rain forest deep woods with tall trees where rain often falls

saint person who lived in a very good and holy way

scuba dive swim under water with air tanks and masks

secondary school school grades 7 to 12

settled moved from one country to live in another country

spice dried, ground-up plant used to flavor foods

sugarcane kind of tall grass that can be made into sugar

surf ride the waves on a special board

tourist person who visits a place while on vacation

# Index